Freefalling...

God's Angels By My Side

The Riveting True Story of One Woman's Documented Path of Pain, Death and God's Miracles

By Linda Diane Worthy

3rd Edition

By Beverly Benson—2020 to Linda Diane Worthy

Table of Contents

Freefalling... God's Angels By My Side
Copyright 2025 by Linda Diane Worthy

Covers and Interior Design by Linda Diane Worthy
YouTube Channel: **@MiraclesAndDance**
Email: **MiraclesAndDance@Gmail.com**
Website: **www.lindadianeworthy.com**

1st Edition (EPub & Paperback)
Edited/Marketed by: Emma Jones of Publish My Book.us

2nd Edition (Hardcover English & Translated to Spanish and Tagalog)
Edited/Marketed by: Katlyn Murphy & Chloe Bennett of Citi of Books

3rd Edition (Hardcover)
Edited/Marketed by: Josh Collins and Ken Ross of Olympus Story House

ISBN: 978-1-969422-24-9 (Paperback)
        978-1-969422-25-6 (Ebook)

Olympus Story House
www.olympusstoryhouse.com

Acknowledgments

- I dedicate this glorious book about miracles and spiritual warfare to **<u>God</u>**, Who first spoke to me in October of 2014, telling me to inform those wanting to pray for my healing, to not do so because You told me You were not going to heal me; instead, for them to pray for strength for the journey ahead. Then, when the 12 year, 4 month spiritual warfare was won, You spoke once again and commanded me to DANCE, and the **<u>Holy Spirit</u>** has guided my every dance step, and to my **<u>Lord and Savior, Christ Jesus</u>**, for dying for my many, many sins, then rising from the dead to become the Lord of my life. I eagerly await to dance on Heaven's streets of gold for all eternity. For twelve years and four months of spiritual warfare, you allowed satan to wage spiritual warfare against me, and allowed me to survive certain death again and again. I praise You for eternity.

- To my husband, **<u>Chuck Worthy</u>**, of 45 years of marriage (married since April 18, 1980) for being there during some very difficult times. It would have been so easy to walk away and yet you did not. I love and appreciate you so very much for all your efforts and concerns. I pray that your published book, *An Honest Christian Poet* (available on Amazon, Kindle, Barnes and Noble, and more), will reach many people with your exquisite gift and blessing of poetry. You are loved and appreciated for all you have done and continue to do.

- To my now deceased parents, **<u>Earl and Beverly Benson</u>**, for your unconditional love, understanding, and prayers for God to send His angels to protect my body from below freezing temperatures that night in March, 2015. I thank both of my parents, especially my dad, for showing me God's heavenly love, paving the way for me to accept a loving Heavenly Father. I have no words to describe your enduring love for me when I went missing for two days in March, 2015. Mom, you stayed up praying that God would send His angels to protect me. Mom, the last gift you ever gave me before your death was the Angel drawing on the back on the front cover of this book. Truer words were never spoken. No one but you and my precious dad could have loved me more.

- To my Primary Care Provider of around 30 years, **Shao-Ti Meredith**, for trusting me and my research, and spending much of your own time helping me to fight the medical system for what my body needed, for your many referrals, for your care and compassion. There is no one like you.

- To **Toyin Adekale**, thank you for being so in tune with the Holy Spirit that, when prompted, you immediately reached out to me and saved my life. You've done so very much for me, including hosting the Podcast on my YouTube Channel: *@MiraclesAndDance*. Toyin, you are an influencer to countless people, but in my heart, you are God's gift to me. My sister in Christ forever.

- To **Linda Lanphere Carpenter Lauritzen**, whom I've known since I was about six years old, for still truly understanding me and providing me laughter, friendship and joy.

- To **Shirley DeFord Keen**, you have been my dear friend and our ministry photographer since the 1990's. God only made one of you, and I am so blessed to call you my friend and sister in Christ. You are a true Proverbs 31 woman!

- To my longtime friend and his wife, **Charles & Kathy Batchelor**. Your generosity in doing my photography has truly blessed me. Your ability to listen, when my other pastoral friends abruptly turned their backs on me, was a great encouragement and blessing at the time. Thank you both!

- To my very beloved nephew, **Barry and Titima Enders** (plus **Ayla**). You were the only one in my family who apologized when it was appropriate (and God knows there were many times I was compelled by Him to apologize to you and the rest of the family). We know the details and will speak no further about it. I love you so much that words are simply inadequate.

- To my "sister", **Margot Ulsh Bowser**. You were always there. Always. Your wisdom helps me cope with the ongoing physical stress and pain. You never lied to me, but wisely spoke the truth. You also helped me to better understand my mom, and I thank you profoundly for that.

- To my special and delightful cousin, **Julie Benson Denmark**. You are living the life most can only dream of, but rarely obtain. We both have treasured memories, and to have you as part of my life is beyond priceless. You are my dear cousin indeed. For life until one day, far too soon, this life becomes eternity.

- To my friend and colleague, **Emma Jones** from Publish My Books. us (1st Edition). Your marketing expertise and drawings with captions are forever priceless. I will always appreciate ALL the work with the website development of *www.lindadianeworthy.com*.

- To my friends and colleagues, **Katelyn Murphy, Zari Castro & Chloe Bennett** from Citi of Books (2nd Edition). You have truly cared about me as a friend, an author and helping me succeed in the wild jungle of publishing. I will never forget you both as I continue to travel through this journey. Thank you from the bottom of my heart.

- To my fantastic dance instructor, **Ally Decker**, with whom I've had the privilege of teaching me to refine the dance God placed in my body. I thought I was a lyrical dancer, but I have since realized, looking back at the videos, that I am an interpretive dancer with no dance ever the same. You are so amazing. You "get" me. We work together, knowing my traumatic brain injury prevents me from memorizing dance steps. What I learn from you, the Holy Spirit then takes my dance steps and movements into something to offer as a gift to God.

- To **<u>Leon Bombardier</u>**, this book would not be possible without your quick obedience to God to run so far while working out in the water and see the top of my head sinking. You grabbed a friend and hurried to drag me from the water's quickly rising tide. You told my dad and husband that the tide was so high it was a miracle you could save me. I totally praise God for you, Leon! I literally owe you and others my very life. I wish God's blessings and joy and strength to move forward until the day He takes His children home. God has blessed me with you with more words than I can say. Thank you.

Foreword by Chuck Worthy

As one who was witness to the events in Linda Worthy's book *Freefalling... God's Angels By Your Side*, I can assure you that these miraculous events are true, well documented, and verifiable.

I'm sure many will be amazed at the sequences of events detailed in *Freefalling*. Spiritual Warfare can take us to mental and emotional places that are beyond our normal experiences. All too often, we think that what we see with our eyes is all that there is. *Freefalling* pierces the veil of the spiritual, allowing us to see the warfare raging all around us.

Freefalling also helps us understand that spiritual attacks can be leveled at anyone. Prior to these events, Linda Diane Worthy was a successful, respected, and sought-after Application Developer. *Freefalling* shows us just how devastating and life-changing spiritual warfare can be and how your world can be shaken to its core. We also see how God can allow such events with a plan to restore and bless you.

Foreword by Linda Diane Worthy

I survived. By the Grace of God, I survived.

Since February, 2011, when a botched sinus surgery left me brain damaged, I still suffer from Traumatic Brain Injury. In mid-June 2023, when, with the mercy and grace of God, HE brought to an end satan's permitted warfare against me. Twelve plus years of intense spiritual warfare. God won. Still, aware/unaware states remain, but mostly benign. Intense pain that puts me in a coma, and my body drops to the floor; later to be found unconscious by Chuck. He would call 911, I would be taken by ambulance to the hospital, and only reading it in my hospital records, did I realize I was in or had been in a coma.

God knew before the beginning of time that I would face this journey. He also knew that, as a little child, my parents (Earl and Beverly Benson) would raise me to accept Jesus into my life at twelve. I subsequently fell away many, many times as a child, teenager, and adult. But God, all knowing, knew I would come out of those twelve years and four months of intense spiritual warfare, and turn back to Him, continuing to praise His name more intensely than ever before. And I do.

God did not reveal this to me until early to mid-February 2024.

Of course, satan failed. He always will. I had many spiritual warriors praying for me when God told me around October 2014 (yes, I heard His voice) to tell people NOT to pray for healing because *He was never going to heal me* (in some ways similar to Paul in the New Testament). Instead, I was to ask others to pray for strength for the journey I would have to endure. I had no idea what that meant. But I believed it. I remember sharing it with a choir rehearsal for the Nativity Choir for the Victorian Country Christmas Fair around October, 2014.

This book is about intense spiritual warfare. And God's mighty triumph. I unwittingly participated, crossing enemy lines. I lost many friends and family.

I went through this spiritual warfare (refer to Addendum A for information on Spiritual Warfare) for over 12 years, and I estimate I lost about three to five years of my life due to being unaware, which inevitably led to God's merciful rescues as shown in this book (not all miracles are included), or sleeping up to twenty hours a day in order to cope with ten years of nonstop and unrelenting intractable pain. It is one of the worst pains known to mankind.

When I was professionally diagnosed by one of the top neurosurgeons, who was a keynote speaker around the world, he told my husband and me that I was so rare that there were, at that time in December 2011, only three or four people with my condition in the world, as was best to his knowledge. He said there is no percentage point for it, as it is too rare, and he essentially told me, at the age of 54, to go home and live the best life I could until I died.

Then, God led me in February, 2021 to a reputable medical website that said a newer medicine I qualified for was available. At a quarterly visit with my doctor, she fought for me to obtain and remain on this newer medicine. Thank you, Shao-Ti Meredith. The pain is no longer constant, but it comes and goes.

You will find in this book a series of highly intriguing miracles; all are true and conclusively documented, even though I was unaware when some of them happened. They are supported by fire department records, medical records, police records, my husband, eyewitness reports, etc. Note that I have not included all the miracles, for there were many. I only included the more major ones.

I pray the reader will be touched, challenged, and ultimately realize that this book is only possible because of God. And that, if needed, they can turn their lives over to God by realizing that God is the giver of ALL miracles.

Why was I chosen? I have no idea. My husband and I, at one time, had been state-wide recognized ministry leaders of Worthy Music Ministries that produced 18 annual Washington State Christian Talent Contests and so much more I cannot list it all. Suffice it to say, we were on the mountain top. I was a highly sought after regional software developer/engineer in the

Puget Sound, which includes Seattle, Tacoma, Bremerton, and many areas both north and southwestern Washington, who had at one time been gifted with an IQ in the top 1 percent.

It has taken me around ten years to write and finish the 1st Edition of this book. It was very painful to dig through years of medical, police, and fire records, only to be reminded of how much damage I caused, regardless of aware or unaware states, to my husband, family, and friends.

My unaware state is mentioned throughout the book. No mental professional has been able to even roughly define it. Some have tried, but all have failed. As my neurological psychologist told me over about seven or eight years of therapy, "You are not mentally ill, but neurologically damaged."

My unaware state is when I am not recording any memories. Think what Ambien can do to people (which I had never used, but the descriptions seemed to closely match what I went through).

I still suffer from unaware states and probably will until I die, but no longer to the same destructive level. I have no memory of what I say or do, although in February, 2020, I read about relatively new technology that exists to retrieve these memories that are not recorded in my memory bank. I have decided to wait until Heaven, when Jesus can wipe away the many tears I will shed, to discover what has been hidden from me for so long.

After suffering twelve years and four months of intense spiritual warfare from February, 2011 to mid-June 2023, I am ready to tell my story.

Background

I had a failed sinus surgery in February, 2011 that left me with trigeminal neuralgia and bilateral trigeminal neuropathic pain, including 24/7 pain. A quick Google of the suicide disease showed me this: *"A diagnosis of trigeminal neuralgia (TGN), commonly nicknamed 'Suicide Disease,' means unpredictable bouts of severe pain that makes everyday living unbearable. Every aspect of life becomes shrouded in currents of unrelenting shocks to the face, causing both physical and mental anguish.* Note that I initially had (and still have) bilateral trigeminal neuropathic pain, then later developed Trigeminal Neuralgia (a cousin).

Worse than chronic pain - it is intractable pain (Google the difference). That started in February, 2011 when the surgeon left bone shavings (the size of a pencil eraser) behind my eye, and I developed a severe facial infection which he never diagnosed or treated in all the follow up visits - until I demanded a post op CT scan, which took place about five weeks following the initial surgery. It showed the major infection and the bone shaving behind my left eye. By then, the damage was done. I was put on heavy-duty steroids to clear up the infection in my face.

I then had a second sinus surgery in April, 2011, about ten weeks after the first surgery, to remove the bone, but nothing helped the pain. Nothing. My meds and pain made it impossible to hold a job (I know - I tried working two different contracts in May through September, 2011) and then I applied for and received Social Security Disability Insurance (SSDI).

I told ALL the doctors and specialists and the ER and the hospitals since 2011 that I was having "blackouts" (even though I don't drink) - now I know that it was some sort of unexplainable amnesia, or as I prefer to call it, my "unaware" state (see Addendum B).

This book shares my incredible series of miracles from documented multiple 100 plus foot falls, blood transfusions, sepsis, kidney failure, comas, and aspirated pneumonia, followed by various doctors exclaiming, "She shouldn't be alive" in my husband's presence at the hospital. Perfect to-the-moment arrival of police, fire department, stranger eyewitnesses, family, and husband clearly proving I was going to die or was already dead, so that each time no one could deny God's perfect timing with His miracles that kept me alive and inspired me to share my riveting miracles of God's grace and power.

That's why Paul said, "If I must boast, I will boast of the things that show my weakness" (2 Corinthians 11:30), and further, "For the sake of Christ, then, I am content with weaknesses, insults, hardships, persecutions, and calamities. For when I am weak, then I am strong" (2 Corinthians 12:10).

Suffering is the root; glory is the flower. Suffering doesn't somehow purchase glory; suffering is glorious. Put another way, glory is what suffering looks like from an eternal perspective. It is the honor of God that crowns God's people.

God made it clear He did not want me healed or for anyone to pray for healing, but rather to pray for strength to endure what was ahead. I had no idea what was to come, and this book speaks of many, many miracles and my surrender to God despite having "one of the worst pain syndromes known to mankind", AKA the "Suicide Disease," in order to give God all the glory.

The book will explain in detail the difference between my aware vs. unaware states, as they are critically important to my book. Suffice it for now that being unaware is where my brain thinks it is asleep and dreaming, even though no one around me can tell. I have no memory of anything, even years later, of what happened while being unaware. The only way I know is by reading police, fire, and hospital reports or hearing them from family and eyewitnesses. My psychologist has explained there is no way to recover what happened because there are no memories in the sense that you can recall what you did earlier that day or had for lunch or dinner. To your mind, it is as though it never happened.

The old forest is about 40 acres of a hidden and destructive death trap. It is more than 200 feet in elevation from top to bottom and ends at the bay, overlooking the Key Peninsula and the Olympic Mountains. It is filled with multiple hidden quicksand traps, and if you step in the wrong place, your body will fall many feet, never to be seen again, even though it looks like solid ground. There are no "paths", and it is indeed a horrible place to find yourself in. My grandfather and father, and later my family, grew up where I now live. The woods are just down the road from my house. My father spent his youth hunting, exploring the "deadly forest". He is now deceased (2018), but he knew those 40 acres quite well.

There were many times that, if God had not sent help within a one-to-five-minute window, I would have died or remained dead. So many times, I DID stop breathing, but it was where either the police, firemen, hospital, eyewitnesses, or Chuck Worthy were at the right place at exactly the right moment in time to save me from certain death. God gets all the credit.

I lost so many friends and family because they refused to believe one of the world's leading neurosurgeons' diagnoses of my exceedingly rare medical condition. He told Chuck and me that he had only heard of a few people like me in the *world*, but I was the first one he had ever met with bilateral trigeminal neuropathic pain (result of failed sinus surgery) and all that went with it. How little did I know?

Why write a book about all my unbelievable yet documented miracles? I've searched for over a decade for a book like mine, and I say this with all humbleness. If you only knew. Seeking but never finding.

But here I am. A truly walking miracle. Around 2022, a MultiCare Orthopedic Surgeon and then a Franciscan Orthopedic Surgeon strongly urged me to use a wheelchair for the rest of my life due to my severe fall history and risk. And yes, someone being unaware of falling 100 plus feet in 2015, breaking my neck, then two years later, being aware while freefalling about 100 feet, breaking my thoracic (mid back) and lumbar (lower back), which didn't even hurt, has a high risk of falls. Due to the agony of bilateral trigeminal neuropathic pain, I was indeed at risk of falling. Such a person should be dead. Praise God for His miracles.

What People Are Saying

"*Freefalling...God's Angels By My Side* is a story to inspire, and regardless of your faith, see what resilience and determination can do. Having witnessed Linda in her ailing days of constant pain, and not being able to walk or at times, enduring excruciating and immobilizing pain yet still holding onto her faith. Her documentation of this journey is a testimony that the impossible for man is not impossible for God.

Whilst I'm not here to impose religion on anyone, it is a wonder to me as a witness to see Linda (who was once unable to stand or walk for short distances or periods of time) dancing with such vibrance and seemingly pain free is something to see. The joy on Linda's face as she floats through her steps interpreting her praise and worship through dance is a mystery.

If you're curious as I am as to how one goes from being crippled in pain, allegedly indefinitely to gliding through a room without restrictions, with steps that emit so much joy then she tells it all in her book. Don't ask me... read the book for yourself."

Toyin Adekale
CEO/President

Talithavoices Entertainment LLC
"Entertainment Tailored to Your Needs"
Official Toyin Adekale Website
"The Crystal City" by Toyin Adekale (A children's book for adults)
"My Mind Wide Open - Surviving Mental Lockdown" - trailer
"The Journey Continues" Album available here
Toyin Adekale Instagram
Toyin Adekale Facebook Page
Talithavoices Facebook

"This book is very educational. I really learned a lot and it was worth my money."
Kimberlee Harris-Kelsey

This is an absolutely inspiring book that shows you God is absolutely on your side no matter what you are going through.
Holly Gonyou

"I received this from a friend and I'm so glad I did. The themes of divine guidance and healing are timeless. A thoughtful gift for anyone struggling with purpose."
William Clark

Linda's storytelling blends divine insight with emotional reality. Some parts felt a bit slow, but the overall message was deeply inspiring and uplifting.
Robert Rodriguez

I wasn't expecting this to move me the way it did. The connection between human experience and divine presence was comforting beyond words.
Mark Nguyen

What struck me most was the honesty in these pages. She doesn't sugarcoat pain or confusion but walks you through it with light and grace.
Anthony Torres

This book feels like a whisper from above. Soft, encouraging, and just what I needed during a rough patch. Would love to read more from the author.
John Ramirez

Linda Diane Worthy shares her harrowing journey through pain, loss, and ultimately, spiritual renewal highlighting the presence of God's angels along the way. Her vulnerability and strength shine through as she recounts miraculous moments and life-changing revelations.

Alleisha

Reading this book shows how you can walk through great difficulties with your faith in God and His love carrying you through. I have known Linda since we were children, and I believe her testimony to be true … the angels by her side were ministering spirits from our Heavenly Father out of His love for her. Angels have been more and more evident in these days!

Lindalee Laughing

Linda captures the complexity of faith in a way that's relatable. Her experiences felt genuine and helped me reflect on my own journey.

Emily Sanchez

If you believe in angels or are exploring your faith, this is must-read. Beautifully written and full of hope.

Daniel Williams

I love this book. It's so refreshing with facts that tell the real story. Its storytelling is lovely, and it speaks to you through words of encouragement and through God. An excellent read!

Sarah

I appreciated how personal this book was. It feels like sitting with a wise friend who has been through spiritual fire and come out stronger. Highly recommended.

Anthony Martin

Linda's tale offers a startling glimpse into a person's journey through excruciating suffering and their courageous demonstration of faith in the face of it all. In her fight she has survived numerous life-threatening situations, giving her a sight of God's kindness that few can match. Her poetry and tale will move you, and you'll discover ways to support people who are experiencing long-term pain.

Shirlisa Kwema Charles

I'm completely swept up in '*Freefalling...God's Angels by My Side*'! This book is an emotional whirlwind that grabbed my heart and wouldn't let go. I adored the characters, was on the edge of my seat with the plot and loved the beautiful storytelling. I laughed, cried, and cheered – it's a true masterpiece. Five stars feels like an understatement – this book deserves so much more!

Pooks

I just finished reading "*Freefalling...God's Angels By My Side*," and it was an incredibly uplifting experience. The author shares personal stories and insights that really resonate with anyone who has faced challenges in life. The way they describe the presence of angels and the comfort they bring is both comforting and inspiring.

The writing style is engaging and easy to follow, making it a quick read. I appreciated how the book combines personal anecdotes with spiritual reflections, which deepens the overall message. It really emphasizes the idea of faith and support during tough times, reminding us that we are never truly alone.

Overall, I would highly recommend this book to anyone looking for inspiration and a deeper connection to their spiritual journey. It's a beautiful reminder of the love and guidance that surrounds us.

Tionna Stevens

See one woman's incredible journey as she falls in the forest, has fractured back; how would she survive without any food supply or cell phone, also dealing with bears, racoons and more roaming wild animals, she was unable to walk, despite that you have to read for yourself. How she somehow made it from the pit to the other steep cliffs down to the water roughly 100 feet below and witness how she is miraculously saved.

Gurpreet Singh

Linda's story is an eye-opening look at someone's journey through extreme pain and the bold testimony of faith they cling to despite it all. She has a glimpse of the mercy of God that few can claim in the many life-threatening experiences she's survived in her battle with bi-lateral trigeminal neuropathic pain.

You will be touched by her story, her poetry and learn how to walk alongside others going through chronic suffering.

Bonnie Foxley,
Published Author

Freefalling…God's Angels by my Side is an inspiring book about one's strength, perseverance and faith in God. You will be moved by her triumphs, her connection and devotion to God and her authenticity in living out her purpose. A work of art directly from Linda's heart and soul.

Alicia S.

I have known Linda Worthy for over 20 years. We met when I was a contestant in 1999 at The Washington Christian Talent Contest. I didn't win anything, yet it didn't matter. It was such a positive and wonderful experience. I was really impressed with both Chuck and Linda, so I started donating my time to help them in the various events they sponsored throughout the Pacific Northwest. They have always been professional, inspiring and talented in their careers along with their passion for music.

I was devastated to find out about Linda's surgery mishap. Then seeing and hearing of some of the trauma she's been through over the years has been really hard...

I believe this book is a wonderful testament of how God can pull us out of the ashes and create such a beautiful life in spite of the tragedy.

I am truly humbled by Linda's steadfastness and continued love for the Lord. I love how music still speaks to her in the graceful and elegant movements of dancing. It is said "Those who don't hear the music think the dancer is mad."

However, I say "LISTEN FOR THE MUSIC AND LIVE YOUR LIFE AS A TRIBUTE TO THE LORD."

Shirley Keen

Linda's book was chilling to read because I remember her experiences like they happened yesterday. To see her live to write a book about it is a miracle itself! If you or someone you know is in a dark place or trial in life, read "Falling...God's Angels By My Side."

Clyde McDade
Author and Filmmaker

Linda Diane Worthy, I've started your book and so far it's great! I already am a subscriber to your YouTube channel. Thank you for the book.

I am so very proud of you. As a documented traumatic brain injury recipient myself, having witnessed your journey, it's amazing to see our lives all come full circle, and you be able to share your story so well while recognizing who the recognition is due. God is so good, and I love you very much Aunt Linda. Everything you told me since I was a little child and through my most difficult times has come true 🙏 Keep up the great work!

Josh Enders
Owner/CEO ProEnd Painting

A gripping true story of miracles that saved Linda Diane Worthy's life. These miracles and her faith in Christ will amaze and inspire you.

Julie D.

Linda Diane Worthy is living proof that miracles happen. She tells the amazing true story in her book, *Freefalling...God's Angels By My Side*. Linda has endured extreme pain and suffering only known by a small fraction of one percent of the world's population. Read how – driven by faith and the Holy Spirit, Linda endured, persevered, and fought off death with God's Angels at her side! I witness and testify to the remarkable healing power that dances through her now."

Doug Miller

Chapter One:
July 14, 2017 - Freefalling

I became aware. My eyes widened as I found myself freefalling in the old forest. Time slowed down. Way down. There was no fear. Intensive medical research over the years states that 100-foot falls will kill you. And they usually take about two or three seconds to complete the fall. Time seemed to stop as I free-fell over 100 feet, feeling like it took several minutes.

With peace, I gently sensed the angels' smooth guidance of my body, veering slightly to the left to an old perc hole for a summer home built in the late 1800s/early 1900s that had somehow morphed into what now looked like a grave.

I landed. Inordinately hard in the back right corner of the hole. Roughly 8 feet long and 4 to 5 feet wide, and a little over 5 feet deep, I had no idea where I was or what had caused me to have freefallen so far down and still be alive. I felt a sharp pain where I fractured my thoracic (mid back) area and my lumbar (low back) area. Even so, as a result of the fall and hard landing, I knew I had to stand up, despite the fractured back pain, to see where I had fallen.

To the front, I saw the sparkling waters and one of the most dazzling blue skies ever as I looked through a plethora of trees between me and the water. Across the water was the Key Peninsula. Lifting my eyes higher, I looked at the splendor of the Olympic Mountains, some with still pristine snow-covered tops. To the left was the gnarled and uneven forest bed, and to my right, I glanced at the strangest tall, grassy weeds I had ever seen. Without warning, I fell on my face with no control, and as my face hit the dirt, my eyeglasses flew. I attempted to evaluate what had happened.

Everything was eerily calm. Still felt peace and serenity until the pain roughly jarred me as it rose steeply in the lumbar and thoracic areas of my back; I was unable to walk or stand. It occurred to me that my back was probably broken from the fall.

In the sweltering heat, I realized there was no way to climb out of my "grave." By verifying with a rough approximation where my broken and now pain-filled body lay, I realized no one was coming. No one knew I had left my property. No one knew where I was.

Bereft, I tearfully considered I would painfully and slowly starve to death. I had no supplies. I didn't even have my cell phone. I could not walk. If I couldn't walk or crawl - and I tried - I knew this hazardous forest contained the homes of bears, deer, cougars, raccoons, and more; how would I survive an attack? It was too shocking. I could not even contemplate the almost certain outcome.

Even if I tried, I could not physically, due to my broken back, crawl out of a five-foot pit that would become my grave. Then what would I do? Even if I miraculously (with, I suppose, the help of the angels I still sensed near me) got my body out of the pit, what then? I still could not crawl or walk. All I knew was I was somewhere in the middle of a precarious forest with no way to get to the road and get help. Death was imminent. No one was coming. My death clock was counting down.

I remember crying out: "God! I want to live!" Mercifully, I once more became unaware.

With no watch or cell phone, there was no way to tell how long l had been out there. The day became relentless in the cloying heat. With gratitude to God, I was still unaware of how I somehow made it from the pit to other steep cliffs down to the water roughly 100 feet below.

How I did so will remain an incredible mystery and miracle, as I could not walk and there was no path. Yet, as God brought me to awareness, I could see I ended up near the water's edge and could see a 100-foot vertical cliff to my right. The tide was coming in, and I had a few feet before the water consumed me. The agony from the barnacles was excruciating as my flesh was penetrated too many times to count. With no other choice, I kept moving forward.

The scorching sun was burning my damaged body with no relief in sight, and the usually cold water was warm and inviting. Feeling total euphoria to be back in the waters of my youth, joy overwhelmed me as my body ignored the crushing pain.

(I later told my dad I could not swim with the tide in the cove. He told me the tide runs backwards in that area. Growing up playing in the pernicious forest, he was an expert. He also informed me that the strange weeds I would have landed in were actually quicksand, where I would have sunk roughly 100 feet to my death had the angels not gently guided my body to the left.)

As I realized I was not making any progress with my swimming endeavors, I winced in utter agony as I carefully crawled back to the shore and collapsed face down on the slicing barnacles. A few feet to my right were vertical cliffs about 100 feet high, and the tide was on my left, roughly two feet away, waiting to take my helpless, broken body and sweep me to a watery death. Again, I went unaware. I did not become aware until more than seven days later in the hospital. All of this. At the age of 61.

The next day, my dad and my husband soon met with the man who saved me. Leon, a retired Jesuit priest, was working on a buoy far out in the water and said it "was a miracle" he could even hear my soft cries for help as I was drowning. He told them he was too far away to normally hear me. I was unaware when I called out for help. He quickly entered the water and called 911. Leon grabbed another friend, running frantically, hoping to find me as I was not visible from such a distance. By now, it was mid-to-late Friday afternoon that day.

Rushing to the water's edge, where I was lying face down, Leon told me he turned me on my side to try and clean out the mud and seaweed debris in my mouth so he could perform CPR until the fire department got there. The ambulance arrived and took me, still unaware, to the hospital.

Here is the published Fire Report from the local paper, the **Peninsula Gateway**, dated July 27, 2017:

"July 14: A property owner of a waterfront property called 911 after finding a woman laying on barnacles and rocks at the water's edge, disoriented, confused, and unable to answer any questions. When crews arrived, they found the woman sitting on some steps at the home, covered in wet clothes and sand, with scrapes and abrasions all over her body. She was unable to answer any questions regarding the events of the day, how she got to the beach, or why she was wet and covered in scrapes. Crews moved her to the medic unit, where her wet clothes were removed, and she was provided a dry gown. She was transported to a hospital for further care."

My husband later shared that I had left our property on foot around noon. Since he was working in his office that day, he had no idea I had not returned. Hours later, he received a call from the Emergency Room. He stated, "When I arrived, Linda was unconscious and was intubated with multiple IV drips applied. At that time, I saw her body covered with bruises, abrasions, and deep scratches. Her body was perhaps 85% covered with cuts and bruises that were overall large, deep, and severe. I could barely recognize her. Her body was swollen as though she weighed perhaps 50 percent heavier."

I had never seen anyone with such injuries. It appeared that she had been systematically beaten with bats, thorny vines, and other instruments of torture. The doctors were also giving Linda IV antibiotics because she had aspirated sea water and had aspiration pneumonia as a result of her near drowning. The medical staff told me they were not sure about the extent of her injuries and how her case would progress because of the severity of those injuries."

When I finally returned home roughly one week later, I became aware again. I had no scrapes, scars, bruises, or any other disruptions to my skin, except for one small barnacle scar God left hidden behind my left eyebrow as a constant reminder of His incredible miracle.

When you consider how the fire department described the damage to my body, and later that night, how my husband described the damage to my body that disappeared without a trace about a week later, I knew that only God could heal my broken body so quickly.

Remember, if you are a child of God, no matter what you may go through, He is always there. He sends His angels, sometimes seen in human form and sometimes invisible, but you can feel them beside you. Only God decides if you live or die, if you are healed or not. Regardless, love and thank Him because HE can see the path ahead and we cannot. He loves you, and although it can sometimes be hard to fully comprehend, He will always be there for you.

Chapter Two:
October 14, 2014 – Angels in Route

I guess the first thing you need to know is the back story (please go to my Forward and Background for more information). This is but one of my miracles, and of all my miracles, it is probably the least dramatic. From my point of view, anyway.

When I became permanently neurologically disabled in February, 2011 from a failed sinus surgery, my life forever changed. I've gone through acceptance and anger that I was "chosen" to undergo what I went through. I was deeply sorrowed at the pain I had inadvertently caused others, especially Chuck, and overall, I still had an acceptance that God is always in control.

On a cold, rainy, and windy early afternoon day on October 14, 2014, I was in terrible pain. My meds were not helping. I took the prescribed dosage, though I have no recollection of doing so. In trying to piece everything together, I can only conclude I was still in intense pain, so I took another dose, not realizing I had already taken a complete dose.

I got worried and called my father (now deceased in January, 2018), who lived next door to us, to come over and get my meds as I was getting concerned I might accidentally overdose, not knowing in my unaware state that I had already overdosed.

He sat and visited for around three hours, not knowing I was already in an overdose state, and neither did I. Still in pain, I handed him all my meds after a couple of hours (Chuck was teaching in his detached office). I did not feel any different. My dad watched me go upstairs to the bedroom, and I remember getting into bed to hopefully sleep my way through the pain. My dad went back home.

Apparently, at some point, while in an unaware state, according to my husband, I got back up and went into my office and started typing. I have no recollection of this.

I must have typed for roughly an hour; about what, I don't recall. At some point, probably from the meds, but sometimes, just due to the terrible pain, I passed out when my head fell on my keyboard. Apparently, there I stayed.

Chuck's poem, *Angels in Route*, and his comments pick up more of the episode. He entered the house, and upon hearing no noise from my upstairs office with the light on, he ran up the stairs. When he realized I was probably dead with no pulse and my eyes rolled back in my head, he called 911, laid my body on the office floor face up, and started very intensive CPR. I guess it took quite a while for me to respond to what was ultimately (and incorrectly) called an intentional overdose/suicide attempt. Believe me, had I not kept going in and out of aware/unaware states, none of this would have happened. According to Chuck, the firemen arrived and gave me a dose of Narcan. I immediately "came to" for a few seconds but could not remain awake.

I understand from that point on, they put me on a gurney and carried me down the stairs to the front door. While I don't recall this, Chuck says I saw him at the door and asked him what he was doing there since I was upstairs asleep in bed? Strange. I guess I got multiple dosages of Narcan because I made it to the ER alive.

I vaguely remember that they kept asking me all these questions, and I kept falling asleep. Normal behavior in my book. I was kept overnight and released the next day.

There are times when, for absolutely no reason at all, I go into an unaware state. Usually no one can tell, not even me, because I usually "virtually" appear, act, and speak the same. I have since undergone intense therapy for it, but it will always be a part of my life. The therapy has just helped me to "contain myself" in an unaware state so I do not get unduly angry, destructive, or harmful, especially to myself. But it does leave you feeling incomplete when there are sometimes days, weeks, conversations, or experiences I cannot account for.

A number of years later, from 2014 until 2021, Chuck shared his poem with me, "*Angels in Route*." It had a profound effect on me, enabling me to "see the light" about how this impacted Chuck. I cannot totally imagine. It must have been a nightmare for him. Then, I was overwhelmed by the sadness of what my family, especially Chuck, had to live through, both during and after some of my non-benign, unaware states.

After Chuck shared his poem, I could only thank God for Chuck's immediate obedience and prayers, giving his life's effort to save mine.

Angels in Route

CEW/10-14-2014
<u>*Shared with permission by Chuck Worthy*</u>

Ring, ringing alarm inside my skull
Up, Son, Up, Go up
Stat! Up, Son, fly now...
On Mercury's wings, I fly
Hero's landing, place of dread

Face down, placid ghoul
What, what have you done
Why, where have you gone
Face down, alphabet face, Drooling

Racing heart, no air
Direction
Up, down to the floor, arms stiff
Just like...
What? Yes, I know, yes, I can...
Yes, I will, Stop The Reaper
Angles in route

My God!! PUSH, PUSH!!!
INTO THE DEAD PUSH LIFE!
Beyond soul death
Rapier in Legion Pierce me

Angels in route
Push, swoosh, push
Real, no TV, no Movie
Push, I am dying

Angles alight
We are here
She is ours
Task is ours

You are here, breathe the air
Angels fly with you
I sit and stare

Chapter Three:
November 15, 2020 – Death of My Mother and Miracles

*"**No!**"* Standing there in stunned silence, I let out a moaning, guttural sound. "No." The word was coming more softly now; I stood there, unable to focus, unable to speak or move as the caller disconnected the call.

Like a little girl lost, my brain refused to comprehend the message.

Having just been informed by my younger brother, John Benson, that my 84-year-old mom (Beverly Benson) had been taken off life support, that no one told me she was even put on, I was left speechless and numb. Disbelief shook my body.

Frozen in place, I solemnly stood at the kitchen counter, barefoot on the cold tile floors, as the hot tears freely cascaded down my face, clouding my focus.

"No." I now agonizingly whispered. *"Oh, Mommy, no!"*

I was not invited as the rest of the family gathered around her for final goodbyes as she was removed from life support. I had no idea until my brother, John, called two hours after the fact.

I couldn't think. I couldn't move. All sense of feeling disappeared into a cesspool of agonizing physical and emotional pain. I gazed out the window at the dreary winter sky filled with falling rain, seeing nothing through my tears.

Roughly wiping away the tears from my growing penetrating bilateral trigeminal neuropathic pain (an extremely rare and incurable condition), I looked down at my kitchen counter. I saw the many vitamins and prescription medications I had yet to take. A little over twenty per day, and I could only take a few at a time.

With agony and growing impatience to just go back to sleep with the hopes this was but a nightmare, I took all my pills in only two or three gulps instead of 2 or 3 pills at a time, unaware that swallowing so many pills at one time would lead to my certain death, had God not intervened.

Once again, God allowed me to go into an unaware state as the last thing I remembered at approximately 2:30 pm on Sunday, November 15, 2020, was taking my medications.

According to my husband, I woke him up around one o'clock am on November 16th. I frantically told him to call 911. He reports I told him in extreme anxiety I was dying. He could see that my words and actions reflected severe panic and high levels of both emotional and physical pain. I remained in total distress as I was unaware when I frantically dressed and packed for the hospital.

Neither one of us knew I was still in an unaware state.

Since I remained unaware since 2:30 pm the prior day, Chuck later told me it took around 15 minutes for the ambulance to arrive. Apparently, I remained highly agitated while they took my vital signs and evaluated me. My blood pressure was unusually elevated, and I was later told that it appeared they believed I was having a major panic attack. My body knew differently.

At their request, Chuck presented the EMTs with my box of medications, and they had me take my prescribed dosage of anti-anxiety meds in an attempt to calm me down, not knowing I had already taken them earlier on Sunday. After some time had passed, they again checked my vitals with improved results.

Even though Chuck said that, in my unaware state, I reported my trigeminal neuropathic pain was extremely high, the EMTs determined that I was in no immediate physical danger. Little did anyone know the deadly occurrences taking place internally were leading me on a path to my certain death.

I stayed unaware through all of this except for approximately one to two minutes when I became aware to electronically sign an agreement not to be taken to the hospital.

Even though Chuck had to be at work in the morning, he stayed awake in the living room while he said I went back to bed.

He listened as I slept. Then, several hours later, he heard strange noises coming from the bedroom. He thought he was hearing loud snoring and didn't think it was a problem.

Not long after, the noise increased in volume, and he realized something was very wrong. When he realized I was having difficulty breathing, even though I was asleep, he attempted to wake me up and found me unresponsive; my body was rigid, and I was soaked in sweat. Chuck again attempted to shake me with no response. He called 911.

When the EMTs returned, they also attempted to wake me up. Although they used several methods, they failed to get any response. They rushed me to the hospital about three miles away. Because of current covid regulations, Chuck was not able to accompany me. I remained unaware until much later that Monday night.

I could not breathe on my own, and the doctors told me they estimated that I had not been breathing for 10 to 15 minutes before being admitted, so they declared in my hospital records I had suffered a traumatic brain injury and multifocal pneumonia (the second cause of death on my mom's death certificate).

Multifocal pneumonia comes from one or more diseases present in more than one location or localized area of the body, such as multifocal pneumonia which infiltrates throughout both lungs.

My elevated troponin level was never explained to me, but medical research shows it could have something to do with my heart.

Aspiration pneumonia is an infection of the lungs. It occurs when saliva or liquid contaminated with bacteria is inhaled (aspirated pneumonia is a serious condition and can be life threatening).

Apparently, when I deviated from taking my meds and vitamins slowly on November 15 and just gulped them down, a number of them ended up in both my lungs, which caused an infection, along with swelling.

I am not sure why I woke up Chuck in the middle of an unaware state during the night and told him I was dying, but I know now it was God. In the meantime, I was growing worse internally as time went on. But no one knew. My discharge vitals showed my oxygen saturation at 90%, worse than when I was admitted, and it was very serious. Due to my oxygen levels not increasing, I was put on 90 days of external oxygen.

They wanted to keep me hospitalized, but after hearing from my brother, John, that my mom died two hours earlier on the morning of December 18th, I let them know I would not stay in the hospital. I was okay using a portable oxygen tank to stay alive. It took almost 90 days for my breathing to return to normal.

I praise God for His miracle of unknowingly waking up Chuck in the middle of the night and for Chuck remaining awake to ensure my breathing was normal, and when it wasn't, Chuck called 911. Had Chuck not done that, and I was unaware and unable to breathe on my own, I would have died. No doubt about it.

If I had not gone to the hospital when I did, I would not have been alive due to my inability to breathe, along with aspirated pneumonia and other internal problems.

Medical info states in part, *"First responders, doctors, nurses, and other healthcare providers should always treat aspiration pneumonia as a medical emergency with a high mortality risk."*

God is a God of miracles. His timing for me has always been right on time, and I give Him all the glory.

Upon my discharge, I was given paperwork. Under 'Why you were hospitalized". It stated: "Your primary diagnosis was Multifocal pneumonia. Your diagnoses also included acute kidney injury, insufficient oxygen in the blood, a disorder of the brain caused by a toxin or poison, abnormal breathing, lactic acid increase, inflammation of lungs due to inhalation of solids and liquids, elevated troponin level, and aspiration pneumonia."

Chapter Four:

March 2015 – "We Regret to Inform You that Your Daughter is Presumed Dead"

I left my home unaware on March 3, 2015, and did not regain awareness until nine days later. I was first found 26 hours later (the evening of March 4) and then transferred from eight days in ICU to acute critical care (ACU). All the while unaware.

The very detailed police report talks about once I was found (26 hours after initially leaving the property) and how hard they tried to raise my core body temp, but could not. Neither could the firemen who came over on the Tacoma Fire Rescue boat on the second night because I could not be taken out by land, only by water. My body's core temperature was on the brink of death. Dark. Darker still the night. No lights and no nearby houses. Just 40 fatal acres of timberland – not flat – quicksand, many dangers. Wild animals. Freezing in 29-degree weather in my light spring jacket. Dark. No memory.

Later, I found out my Mom prayed for God to send His angels to protect me as I could not be found. Everything is in His timing, so only HE can get the glory. I am sure the Angels were there to soften my landing as most people die upon hitting the ground after falling straight down 100 plus feet.

After searching with the police and their dogs, they returned to my parents' home, where the family was gathered. They told my family I could not survive the below freezing, cold weather that night, and my mother told me she prayed that God's angels would cover my body with enough warmth to keep me alive.

I was unaware. I did not move. I did not know at that time that I was kept frozen in place by God. Upon leaving the hospital, the orthopedic surgeon showed my husband and me that my C5 (neck region) was broken in two places and should have been a solid break. He said it was a miracle I wasn't completely paralyzed. He showed my husband and me CT scans of my neck, showing I missed becoming a quadriplegic by 1/8th of an inch.

I praise God for His divine mercy and unconditional love. What an amazing God. Several years ago (around 2021), at different times, two Orthopedic surgeons told me I should never walk again because I was a major fall risk. They said this when they wanted me only in a wheelchair. No! I refused and continued to fall over and over again.

March, 2015. It was a location in the woods overlooking the water, not far from my house, and as a kid, my brother, John and I played in that area where there was an old summer house and dump where my brother, John, would look for old bottles, and I would look for other antiques.

The police didn't want to bother uncrating the dogs based on my brother's epiphany, even with exact GPS coordinates, as they had been searching the second day unsuccessfully with the dogs. So they told my Mom, "We regret to inform you that your daughter is presumed dead". Oh, how little did they know the plans God had in store for me!

At my brother's insistence, since he knew where I was, they finally uncrated the dogs and went to the area my brother said I was in. I guess my brother told the police that if they didn't go, he would go himself. So, they went and took the dogs.

One dog team had two dogs, and the other had one dog. The two dogs went in the wrong direction, according to the detailed police report.

But one dog refused to leave the top of a cliff. My body could not be seen, but the police officer yelled my name, and I responded, still unaware. The police could not find a way down to where I was, so they had to go a great distance to go around the fallen trees and 100-year-old ferns in the dark (over about 130 feet down a deadly cliff).

When they finally got there, I had just stopped breathing. A minute or so later, I would have been dead from lack of oxygen, and CPR would not have worked. God is known for His perfect timing. This was one of those occasions. They were able to get me breathing again, just in time.

When the Tacoma Fire Rescue Boat arrived, they, too, tried to move my body core temperature above death's level but could not. All these heroic measures were captured in detail in the police report, which I still have.

The Tacoma Fire Rescue Boat got me five miles across the water to the Purdy Spit/Bridge and transferred me to a waiting ambulance, where I was taken to St. Joseph's Hospital in Tacoma.

I arrived at the ER with severe hypothermia. They put me in a metal neck brace. I then died in the ER, but they were able to bring me back.

Had I been found even minutes later, I would have died outside the ER and not been able to be brought back to life. Had the police not gotten to my dead body and brought me back to life just in time, I would be dead. My body had shut down and was ready to die, and it did. Thank God I have no memory of any of that. Still, I did die multiple times that night, brought "back" due to the grace of God, who breathed life into me. These were not "near death" experiences. They are documented by police and hospital records for what they were.

They spent a week trying to save my life in the ICU. I had acute kidney failure. I needed a blood transfusion. My entire body was grossly swollen and stayed that way for a week. Internally, my organs had already begun the shutdown process of dying. It was touch and go.

My family had been praying since I went missing the afternoon of March 3 (I was found on March 4 in the evening) that God would send His angels to protect me and to keep me from freezing to death since it froze that night. Their prayers were answered! It was a true miracle because no one should have survived the approximately 130 foot fall. No one should have survived so many hours in below freezing temperatures. God is merciful.

I truly believe the angels cushioned my fall and then hovered over my body to keep me alive when the temperature dropped to below freezing that night. There are wild animals in those woods, and I was left alone by them. It was low tide, or I might have ended up in the water (as it was, I ended up about eight feet from the water on a slightly risen platform the water could not touch) and I could not have survived in the water at all as the tide would have carried me to my grave.

I was also diagnosed with radial nerve palsy because I had landed on my right arm (and laid on it for probably most of the two days I was missing).

It was grossly swollen (but so was my entire body that first week) and they didn't realize for a week that I had no use of my right arm or hand. Of course, by the time Chuck noticed and brought it to their attention, I had become "aware", and my amnesia was gone. Think of a stroke victim's hand, how it hangs at the wrist and is curled into a fist. That's how my right hand was, and they told me after a very painful procedure, the nerve conduction test, it would scientifically take a year or more to have my right arm, wrist, hand, or fingers return to normal functioning. Scientifically, yes. In God's timing, no. Six weeks later, I had full use of my right hand and arm. Only God.

Unfortunately, I did damage my right knee in the fall (I did NOT need more pain in my total knee replacement from December 19, 2014!) and I needed a third surgery in June 22, 2015 (3 surgeries in 11 months on the same knee!). I still experience pain in my right knee, but I can mostly manage it. I must admit, my doctor from OPA Ortho in Seattle, Dr. Jason King, was quite the miracle worker!!

Through it all, I can see God's hand at work. It was a miracle - all the way around. I cannot imagine the grieving that my family went through. I should not have lived. And yet I did. I still have terrible, terrible pain from my failed sinus surgery and my bilateral trigeminal neuropathic pain in my face. I am neurologically disabled.

In April, 2015, Chuck, my brother John, and I went down to the area where I fell from. Chuck tried to get to the landing eleven feet down and fell. Fortunately, he was able to stop himself before he went over the edge like I did in March. But even after seeing the area and seeing how easy it was to trip getting down to the landing, it didn't bring back any memory of the fall. It is gone from my brain forever. All my amnesia/unaware state experiences are totally gone.

My Hospital Records from March 2015 Show:

The high probability of sudden clinically significant deterioration in the patient's condition required my highest level of medical decision making and my highest level of preparedness to intervene emergently. The patient was re-evaluated and reexamined multiple times during the visit.

- Critical condition
- Cervical collar
- Coma
- Hepatic encephalopathy
- Encephalitis
- Hypernatremia
- Hyponatremia
- Intracranial hemorrhage
- Hypoglycemia
- Meningitis
- Seizure and postictal state
- Sepsis
- Status epilepticus
- Subarachnoid hemorrhage
- Subdural hematoma
- Uncal herniation
- Renal insufficiency
- Cervical spine fracture
- Respiratory failure
- CPT codes 99291 and 99292
- Multiple abrasions on extremities and face
- Decreased oxygenation.
- Respiratory failure requiring intubation (HCC)A
- Radial nerve palsy
- Nerve conduction study
- Fracture of cervical vertebra C5
- Acute renal failure/renal insufficiency
- Respiratory acidosis
- Rhabdomyolysis (often called rhabdo) was treated aggressively with IV fluids and intubated with anesthesia. It is a serious medical condition

that can be fatal or result in permanent disability. Rhabdo occurs when damaged muscle tissue releases its proteins and electrolytes into the blood. These substances can damage the heart and kidneys and cause permanent disability or even death.

- Hypothermia
- Radial nerve palsy, abnormal study
- Spent extended time on the right arm causing extrinsic pressure leading to radial nerve damage

Through all my sufferings and all my unbelievable, but heavily documented miracles, I am only alive and functioning because of God. The Giver of all miracles. My Lord and Savior. May I never take these eyes off Jesus. He and He alone deserve my honor, my love, and my praise.

I don't know why He has so openly blessed me with years of His miracles. I did nothing to earn or deserve it. I praise God for everything I went through during this most horrendous (in America) spiritual battle that consumed twelve years and four months of my life. I lost almost everything, showing that, in the end, only Jesus matters.

Chapter Five:
June 2023 – The Miracle of Dance

God reached out one month before I turned 67 in June, 2023 and told me to **<u>DANCE</u>**. (Note: This is the first time since October 2014 that I have actually heard His voice.) I thought, I have never danced a day in my life or wanted to. I am actually disabled and suffer from documented Traumatic Brain Injury, Bilateral Trigeminal Neuropathic Pain, and Trigeminal Neuralgia. Plus in October, 2025 I will have a total right hip replacement (by Dr. Jason King, of course!).

I can't memorize dance steps. Thankfully, the Holy Spirit guides my footsteps, even though I was told by two orthopedic surgeons around 2021 never to walk again due to my high fall risk. However, God blessed me with this oh-so-joyful thing called interpretive dance. I believe He did so to celebrate the twelve years and four months of some of the worst and long-lasting spiritual warfare (in America). Other parts of my book explain this in a lot of detail.

I still (third quarter, 2025) suffer and can sometimes barely walk and sometimes still get dizzy, but when I practice, rehearse, or perform, God keeps His promise to guide me with zero pain. The healing is only when I am practicing, rehearsing, or performing. Then I go back to being disabled again. Each dance is a true and living miracle to what God has so graciously blessed me with.

When God woke me up, telling me to dance, for a few moments, I was in disbelief. Kind of like Sarah from the Old Testament. I'm too old, my body too broken, and two different orthopedic surgeons wanted me to spend the rest of my life in a wheelchair. How could I dance? I believe the Holy Spirit reassured me that if God commands it, then He will make a way. My Traumatic Brain Injury prohibits my brain from memorizing dance steps, so I literally step on the dance floor, trusting my steps to the Holy Spirit.

I was also quietly assured I would dance with the strength of a woman in her 30s (I recently turned 69 this past July, 2025), and that I would never have pain while dancing. God/Holy Spirit would literally guide my footsteps so I would never fall.

Following are some photos taken by Charles R. Batchelor from my various performances from 2023 to 2024.

Chapter Six:
March 2025 – God Is Not Done With Me Yet

This miracle in Chapter Six was not included in the 1st edition of my book, *Freefalling...God's Angels By My Side,* because this happened after the 1st edition had been published.

I erroneously thought that, OK, I have lived and survived all these years with God blessing me with miracle after miracle. But God let me know, He is NOT finished with me yet.

Around January, 2025, I went unaware during the night. I apparently went out to the living room and sustained a very bad fall, unaware. The next morning, I could not use either arm from my elbows to shoulders.

Having had surgery in 2008 for a right arm only Shoulder Impingement Syndrome, I knew what had happened to me. Somehow, in an unaware state, I tripped (nothing to trip on) and fell hard. I apparently put out both arms to break the fall. The next morning, I knew something had happened when I could not use my arms.

I went through the process of x-rays, then MRI's. They showed I did indeed need surgery. On February 3, 2025, I showed the MRI results to my physical therapist. Suddenly, I felt this strange sensation in my shoulders. In front of my physical therapist, I moved my arms in ways that are impossible for someone who had documented (via MRI and exam) shoulder impingement syndrome. My therapist fell silent.

I calmly said, "Well, you've just seen a miracle." He agreed and documented it all in my physical therapy records. When I got home, the orthopedic surgeon's office called to schedule my surgery.

I told them I would not be having the surgery and why. She put it in my medical records. I told them why and they documented my miracle in my medical records, plus my Primary Care Provider documented it in my medical records at Evergreen Health in Redmond, Washington. Again, another documented miracle.

And as usual, I asked God, "Why me?" I didn't get a direct answer except a strong feeling that God still has much work to do in my life.

Addendum A:
Spiritual Warfare

(Note: much is not my writing because I got it from the internet and failed to take note to give proper credit)

According to Wikipedia, "*Spiritual warfare is the Christian concept of fighting against the work of preternatural evil forces. It is based on the biblical belief in evil spirits, or demons, which are said to intervene in human affairs in various ways.*"

More important is what God's Word says, as the Apostle Paul writes:

Ephesians 6:10-18 (New International Version)
10. Finally, be strong in the Lord and in His mighty power.
11. Put on the full armor of God so that you can take your stand against the devil's schemes.
12. For our struggle is not against flesh and blood, but against the rulers, against the authorities, against the powers of this dark world, and against the spiritual forces of evil in the heavenly realms. (emphasis mine)
13. Therefore, put on the full armor of God so that when the day of evil comes, you may be able to stand your ground, and after you have done everything, you can stand.
14. Stand firm then, with the belt of truth buckled around your waist, with the breastplate of righteousness in place,
15. and with your feet fitted with the readiness that comes from the gospel of peace.
16. In addition to all this, take up the shield of faith, with which you can extinguish all the flaming arrows of the evil one.
17. Take the helmet of salvation and the sword of the Spirit, which is the Word of God.

18. And pray in the Spirit on all occasions with all kinds of prayers and requests. With this in mind, be alert and always keep on praying for all the Lord's people.

If we could only see the spiritual battles taking place. It's absolutely real. And through it all, even when I would literally think, today is the day I cannot live anymore, I often feel someone is right then actually praying for ME. My Spirit is so in tune with the prayers being prayed at specific times.

This brings to mind my dear Sister in Christ, Toyin Adekale, who felt the prompting of the Holy Spirit one day years ago, and she called me in obedience to the Holy Spirit. She had no idea how critical a time it was for me. Laying alone in bed in some of my worst pain (*see Addendum D. Comparative Pain Scale*), I felt like I could not make it one more day.

I daily underwent such severe pain and, with no end in sight and no understanding from anyone, I was in the midst of an intense spiritual battle. One day, in particularly horrendous pain, I once thought, "Well, you just got your prescriptions refilled. You have enough to end this pain once and for all."

At that very moment, Toyin Adekale (*Google her*) called me. I remember reluctantly answering the phone. That moment changed my plans. Toyin talked with me. I can't recall what she said, but by the end of the conversation, she prayed with me. I stayed in bed with renewed hope, and as I recall, God allowed me to have a deep and pain-free sleep. Thank you, God, and thank you, Toyin, for being obedient to the Holy Spirit.

My point in the above paragraph is to strongly emphasize that if the Holy Spirit puts someone on your heart, drop what you are doing (if possible) and get in contact with them, or at least pray for them. God knows the details. You may never know that God is sending YOU to someone hurting, sad, or desperate; your obedience could actually save a life in the name of Jesus. NEVER shrug it off (as I have often done) and think you will do it later. Thank God Toyin obeyed that very moment.

I BEG all of you who are Christians to heed that small, still voice of the Holy Spirit and boldly pray immediately. God may or may not tell you who or what to pray for, but please pray the exact moment He puts it on your heart.

Mighty battles are happening to me and many others. Sometimes, I am too weak to pray, but I know with all my heart and soul that God is prompting someone to pray. Please be that person. Sometimes, I cannot pray because my body literally feels like I am dying. I have felt it. My Spirit feels your prayers for this weakened warrior. I know I am not alone.

When I got my diagnosis on December 13, 2011, I was told there was no hope and to try to live the rest of my life, at age 55, the best I could. It is only through God's will and my prayer warriors, many of whom I don't know, that have kept me alive, even through the most horrendous things that should have physically killed me multiple times. Chuck Worthy would sit with me in a coma for seven or eight days in the ICU while they tried to save me and then five or six days in Acute Critical Care. He heard doctor after doctor remark, ***"She should not be alive."*** I never heard this because I was either in a coma or an unaware state. How grateful I am to my husband, Chuck Worthy, whom I married 45 years ago (April 18, 1980 to April 18, 2025) and counting.

I had kidney failure that took five days to repair in the ICU (Intensive Care Unit). Pneumonia. Liver damage. Blood transfusions. Comas. Sepsis. Yet, although the hospital did not believe I would live, as they fought five hard days to save my life, God gets all the glory. Almost every day of my life since my failed sinus surgery in February 2011 to February 2021, when I researched and found a newer medicine that my doctor, Shao-Ti Meredith, prescribed, I suffered from the worst intractable pain for ten years (*see Addendum D on the Comparative Pain Scale*). Since my new medicine, I am mostly okay, although I do have periods that last 4 or 5 days with non-stop pain. I average 15 to 20 hours of sleep in a 24 hour period.

Do not hesitate to pray whenever prompted, even if you don't know who or what you are praying for. I am only alive because of God's mercy and at least one or more people praying. Even then, multiple doctors said **I should not be alive**.

I was supposed to be a quadriplegic after falling over a hundred foot plus cliff while totally unaware, with only 1/8th inch to keep me from being a quadriplegic (as Chuck and I were shown my MRI from the orthopedic surgeon in March 2015). Left to die overnight when the temperature got below freezing. The police and dogs could not find me and told my family they would be back the next day to try and find my body (*see Chapter Four*).

I would like to firmly say to any Christian reading this: DO NOT HESITATE TO PRAY when God prompts you. Not even for a minute. You may never know the results of your prayer, but God does. Spiritual battles rage every day. People's lives may literally hang by a thread, angels standing strong, waiting for YOUR prayer at that very moment.

Addendum B:
My Unaware vs. Aware States

This addendum is taken from sessions I had as homework assignments from one of my therapists regarding my upbringing, childhood, early adult years, and current therapy (from 2017 to 2022). This text is me writing directly to my therapist, and in sharing these, I open up to you, the reader, with total honesty that can be rare at times from some authors. Realizing this may be difficult for the reader to read, I nevertheless have included it as a truly honest look into my psyche both as a child and adult, and later a brain damaged older adult. These are, of course, no longer significant issues in my life, but they do represent the tortuous years from 2011 to 2021 when my intractable, extraordinary, and rare pain ruled my life.

Would there have been a different outcome were I not living in the same place where I grew up? Probably. But I am unable to comprehend it. Personally, it doesn't seem to affect me, although it might.

I felt like everyone failed me. I felt harshly judged by the mental professionals who never took any time to know me; they just quickly labeled me without any attempt to uncover the truth. I subconsciously and sometimes consciously hated them for failing me.

With complete truthfulness, I believe you (my therapist) have properly placed the anchors in my brain for my awareness to control the angry, unaware me. That is why on the night my precious father died (January 8, 2018) my little girl, unaware state, had to approach my adult aware state for permission to "take a walk" (which meant endangering my life). She begged and pleaded. Thanks to your carefully placed anchors, the adult me denied the angry and sobbing little girl. Me.

I was never "multiple personalities," and I believe you (my therapist) recognized this early on. I felt professionally cared about and, most importantly, believed, and therefore I entrusted, to the extent I was able, the angry little girl unaware state to you while despising almost all the other professionals I had seen but failed to believe or help me.

So, million-dollar question. How do we move forward? I believe I have, for the most part, done as much as possible. Regardless of if I remember it or not, the angry little girl is probably quite often denied by the rational, aware adult me. The fact that I have been able to analyze myself and reach these conclusions is quite reassuring.

It convincingly calms me to accept that I no longer fear my unaware state. I know when she emerges, I must go to bed. Go to sleep. Take away her control or constant pleading, as it both fascinates me and repels me. I will admit I have a certain amount of satisfaction in being able to do what I hope is clear and concise thinking regarding my aware vs. unaware state accomplished so much. It is not complicated at all. But it HAS been a very troublesome issue for me. I feel so much calmer understanding that little girl trapped into a time frame of society where I had to "assume society's mask" to succeed can now be intimately understood by me, aware or not (this would probably not be true for me had I been born into a later generation).

This is a huge part of my healing. Due to my personality, it has been critical for you (my therapist) to guide the way toward me understanding the angry, unaware state and knowing how to deal with that little girl. I must also admit that I am quite pleased to be able to articulate (at least to my understanding) this scenario to the extent I am able.

I realize now that being well liked among my teachers and other authority figures (in and outside of the school, church, military, and life beyond the Navy) was simply a reflection of this socially acceptable precept that has been a deep, complex part of my life for as long as I can remember. From a young age, I had a role to play, and I played it well. Very well. However, in many instances, I was not allowed to be myself because being "me" meant going against this deeply ingrained precept.

I grew up as the peacemaker in the family, as well as a well-liked child who befriended the children who had no friends. Rarely did I get in trouble.

I look back and realize I did several things to cope. I did not dwell on it. I also submerged that angry little girl very, very deep into my subconscious.

Because I was highly intelligent, I knew this wasn't fair, and it wasn't right. I knew I worked so hard to be perfect, but I was angry I could never be perfect enough.

To stay out of trouble, and beyond that – to make my mother proud – was a crucial part of my role in childhood. One I carried over into adulthood. My successes as a child, a teenager, a young adult in the military, and finally, as a young adult to middle-aged adult to now at the age of 68, all focused around that one precept. Socially acceptable.

My countless high profile state-wide successes in the ministry (Worthy Music Ministries) brought my parents unbelievable pride.

The military also helped me push back the "real me" because there can be terrible consequences if you display your true feelings or anger. Perhaps that is why I fit in so well in the Navy.

This is a very long-winded background, but it takes the reader to the present day as it does support my theory of my aware vs. unaware state. Yes, the failed sinus surgery and ensuing infection resulted in lasting traumatic brain injury. Still, I believe innately, obviously without training, that there are two types of my unaware state.

There is the benign unaware stage, where no one around me can tell I am either in or just coming out of an unaware state. I simply cannot recall anything I said or did, or was said or done to me, during these benign times. I am on autopilot, and it closely mirrored my own image and hidden emotions from childhood.

Then, there is the non-benign unaware state where that angry little girl emerges from the deepest levels of my consciousness. Hidden away for decades. She is angry. Oh, so angry. And no one can stop her. When we add unbearable, intractable, untreatable pain to the mix, bad things happen. Subconsciously, this angry little girl knew these feelings and actions were wrong. However, as she did when she was a child, she escaped to the woods. The woods and waters of her childhood. It was a place of her natural retreat as she was growing up. Unfortunately, her older, damaged body did not navigate the woods now with the ease of being a strong child, hence the resulting physical trauma.

Over the years, which has become a huge part of my life, to the extent I used to ruminate about this almost daily, to the extent I've been able (totally untrained) to try hard to understand this part of my life, I can finally put it into "words". I finally recognized her. She is me at about five to eight years old. Very intelligent, very well trained, very well mannered, very well-liked by school teachers and church adults, and was even given very special privileges no one else received even when I served in the Navy. Everything in my life centered around the precept of "Socially Acceptable."

Addendum C:
Poetry Throughout Journey

I have been writing poetry since the tender age of eight, when my first poem was published in the Artondale Elementary School paper in 1964. Poetry, then later songwriting, has been a large part of my artistic development. It is natural that I turned to poetry during this very confusing and complex time of what I now know to be twelve years and four months of intense spiritual warfare.

Some poems are questioning, others are more neutral, and some are very dark. Nevertheless, this was part of how I documented this journey that took over ten years to write the 1st Edition.

These are not listed by topic or in any kind of order, except the first one was written when, following that incredibly destructive sinus surgery; for the first time in my life, I had no idea regarding who I was and how I fit into society anymore. The photo was taken by Chuck on our property with a glorious rainbow in the background. Obviously, to Christians, rainbows carry very significant thoughts about them.

Who Would You Be

Who would you be if you were me
Your pain stripping clear your identity?

You'd look the same, you'd talk the same
But unbearable pain—it is no game.

Your profession gone, your passion dead
But it's "just pain", it's "all in your head".

And yet you try each passing day
To wear your mask to hide your pain.

What is left when "you" aren't there,
And debilitating pain is everywhere?

Pick up the pieces, do as best you can;
God's in control, He does have a plan.

It's hard to know, harder yet to believe,
Yet I know He's there in ways I can't conceive.

The power of prayer has kept me strong;
The faith of so many cannot be wrong.

And yet, who *would* you be
If you were me?

I Corinthians 10:13
No testing has overtaken you except what is common to mankind. And God is faithful:
He will not let you be tested beyond what you can bear, but when you are tested,
He will also provide a way out so that you can endure it.

35

Never Be Free

(November 26, 2017)
by Linda Worthy

Words you dare not speak
Things you must not do
Expectations push emotional boundaries
Yet you dare not fail

Perfection, disguised as you
Demanding all you are
Real or not
Perception of perfection
Defines your role

Quick, hide that expression
Assume society's mask
Your persona presents
That which is expected
Demanded
All else is punished

Socially acceptable
Lives to rule another day
You will never be free.
Longing to Believe (February 2018)
By Linda Worthy

Loneliness abates as emotional pain recedes
Into a tuneless melody fading out,
Words long since forgotten.

I look around, seeing slivers of reminders
Of pain, despair, and abandonment
Evaporate quietly in the darkening shadows.

I turn to face the man beside me,
Gazing with glorious wonder as he takes my hand
Holding me close, he strokes my hair
And gently tells me the dark night is over.

And I long to believe.

Miracles

(December 31, 2017)
by Linda Worthy

I've lived, I've died
Unawareness surrounding me
Falling hard 100 feet
I cannot be seen
Will I ever be found?
No memory of unrelenting pain
Broken neck, cannot move
Held hostage in the totality of darkness
Bordering on a full moon

No lights on the contentious water
No movement in the darkened forest
Save the faint whisper of angel wings
Lingering over my battered body
Sustaining me with their touch of life
And the warmth of heavenly wings

Missing. Twenty six hours in freezing cold
Body shutting down, prepared to die
Unaware no help was coming
Unaware of endless searching
Family, neighbors, police, dog teams
Parents praying for God's angels
To keep me safe
Even while preparing
For my inevitable death

The power of prayer is stronger
His miracles are greater
Then, the grasp of death.

The Daisy

(November 2019)
by Linda Worthy

Brilliant sunshine gently caresses her weary back;
Sitting like a child on the grass
Life seems so calm, so uncomplicated
To the busy people
Walking quickly through the park.

She casually observes a lone daisy
Growing quietly amongst the uncut grass.
Like a naughty child, she reaches out to pluck it
To set it free because she is not free.

Gently holding it in her grown up hands
He loves me
He loves me not
No. You already know the answer.

Slowly, unaware of her tormented surroundings,
Her eyes glaze over the unseen beauty.
With no thought of her actions,
She slowly and methodically resumes her plucking.
Do I live?
Do I die?

She hesitates as her damaged soul attempts to grasp
What she found in forbidden territory
Live?
Die?
Live?
For what?

Why put this weight on an innocent weed?
Her mind wanders as her fingers continue to
Slowly pluck the dying daisy.
Live?
Die?
Live?
Die?

Who cares?
Coin toss or pluck the petals
The method makes no distinction.
What will be, matters not.

She closes her exhausted eyes
As unbidden memories flood
Her confused and broken heart.
Live?
Die?
Is there really any choice?

She struggles to rise from the damp earth,
Walking directly to her car.
Driving despairingly home
Knowing another daisy
Waits for her decision
Tomorrow.

Hope Reborn
(November 2017)
by Linda Worthy

The deeper the valley
the more glorious the climb
To leave shadows behind
reaching for ribbons of sunlight

Seemingly impossible
To push past despair
As everyone mocks you
love forsakes your essence

Defying the odds
Push forward with hope
Forgive where need be

Trust God He is stronger
To heal your heart
Tears wiped away
Your pain expunged
Let love soothe your soul.

Feel hope reborn.
For better or worse.

Weary

(November 14, 2017)
by Linda Worthy

I stand alone
A weary traveler
Lacking a compass
To guide my feet

While I still breathe
There is yet hope
While I still walk
I will move forward

Look behind me
No one follows
The path is empty
As night draws near

Chilled, my body
Pushes onward
Drawing on courage
I thought was dead

The night is long
But I am stronger
No fear, no dread
Confidence restored

I start to run
Flushed with hope
Secure I can do this
As my path unfolds.

Endless Pain

(2016)
<u>By Linda Worthy</u>

Love once so strong
Beauty destroyed
By burning endless pain
Fearful
Hurting
Crying out for love
No one there
To care
If you live or die

What does it matter
Family, friends
Cannot, will not
Accept that pain
Changed forever
In the blink of an eye

Pain pushes forth
A bully
A destroyer
Forever changed by relentless pain
You know you will die
By pain forcing your hand
So painful to lose
Everything that matters

Pain, fierce and demanding
Destroys love and life
Far better to
End it now
Than to be an empty shell
Pitied and despised
By everyone you love.
There is no hope
When endless pain
Has destroyed
All you ever were
And what you will
Never again achieve
A broken shell
Devoid of love
Frees those shackled
By duty and obligation
Love once thought eternal
Dies with the brave soul

Fragile Hope

(2015)
by Linda Worthy

Fragile Hope
Elusive Hope
Escapes my soul
Drifting, wandering
Questioning life

Endlessly hoping
That life would be different
And shattered hope renewed
But it is hard to hold

For hope is fragile
Escaping definition
And cannot exist
Without encouragement

I long to hope
I dream of hope
But fragile hope
Can be fleeting at best

Leaving me dry, empty
Questioning with despair
Confused, then angry
When hope is not there

How long can I wait
How much more must I do
Nothing is good enough
And finally fragile hope is broken

Addendum D:
Comparative Pain Scale

Comparative Pain Scale

	0	No pain. Feeling perfectly normal.
Minor Does not interfere with most activities. Able to adapt to pain psychologically and with medication or devices such as cushions.	**1** **Very Mild**	Very light barely noticable pain, like a mosquito bite or a poison ivy itch. Most of the time you never think about the pain.
	2 **Discomforting**	Minor pain, like lightly pinching the fold of skin between the thumb and first finger with the other hand, using the fingernails. Note that people react differently to this self-test.
	3 **Tolerable**	Very noticable pain, like an accidental cut, a blow to the nose causing a bloody nose, or a doctor giving you an injection. The pain is not so strong that you cannot get used to it. Eventually, most of the time you don't notice the pain. You have *adapted* to it.
Moderate Interferes with many activities. Requires lifestyle changes but patient remains Independent. Unable to adapt to pain.	**4** **Distressing**	Strong, deep pain, like an average toothache, the initial pain from a bee sting, or minor trauma to part of the body, such as stubbing your toe real hard. So strong you notice the pain all the time and *cannot completely adapt.* This pain level can be simulated by pinching the fold of skin between the thumb and first finger with the other hand, using the fingernails, and squeezing real hard. Note how the similated pain is initially piercing but becomes dull after that.
	5 **Very Distressing**	Strong, deep, piercing pain, such as a sprained ankle when you stand on it wrong, or mild back pain. Not only do you notice the pain all the time, you are now so preoccupied with managing it that you normal lifestyle is curtailed. Temporary personality disorders are frequent.
	6 **Intense**	Strong, deep, piercing pain so strong it seems to partially dominate your senses, causing you to think somewhat unclearly. At this point you begin to have trouble holding a job or maintaining normal social relationships. Comparable to a bad non-migrane headache combined with several bee stings, or a bad back pain.
Severe Unable to engage in normal activities. Patient is disabled and unable to function independently.	**7** **Very Intense**	Same as 6 except the pain completely dominates your senses, causing you to think unclearly about half the time. At this point you are effectively disabled and frequently cannot live alone. Comparable to an average migraine headache.
	8 **Utterly Horrible**	Pain so intense you can no longer think clearly at all, and have often undergone severe personality change if the pain has been present for a long time. Suicide is frequently contemplated and sometimes tried. Comparable to childbirth or a real bad migraine headache.
	9 **Excruciating Unbearable**	Pain so intense you cannot tolerate it and demand pain killers or surgery, no matter what the side effects or risk. If this doesn't work, suicide is frequent since there is no more joy in life whatsoever. Comparable to throat cancer.
	10 **Unimaginable Unspeakable**	Pain so intense you will go unconscious shortly. Most people have never experienced this level of pain. Those who have suffered a severe accident, such as a crushed hand, and lost consciousness as a result of the pain and not blood loss, have experienced level 10.

http://www.tlpna.org/info/documents/ComparativePainScale.htm

Addendum E:
19 Things People With Chronic Pain Want You To Know

I am not the author of this. Years ago, while searching on the internet, I came across this. It was a person with Trigeminal Neuralgia, a cousin of my Bilateral Trigeminal Neuropathic Pain diagnosis, and was dated December 17, 2015. Although it was written for the most common type of pain, Chronic Pain, it also applies to people like me diagnosed with Intractable Pain (diagnosed in November 2011 by the Assistant Professor of Neurosurgery at the University of Washington Medical School).

The definition of Intractable Pain: Intractable pain refers to a type of pain that can't be controlled with standard medical care. Intractable essentially means difficult to treat or manage. This type of pain isn't curable, so the focus of treatment is to reduce your discomfort. The condition is also known as intractable pain disease or IP.

1. If we had the choice, we would never cancel plans.
2. Our illness won't just go away. It isn't a cold.
3. We don't know how to answer you when you ask us if we're feeling better yet. Because we aren't...and we might never be.
4. Sometimes, all we need is to just know you are here for us.
5. We have exhausted all resources, so if there was a cure, we would know about it. But thank you for trying and finding holistic cures.
6. We're trying very hard to lead a normal life.
7. Some days, it's a struggle just to get out of bed. But on other days, we feel as if we could run at least part of a marathon!

8. We have a difficult time explaining how it feels to suffer from chronic pain.

9. We need a lot of sleep.

10. Please, please do not tell us that someone, somewhere, has it worse than we do. That only makes us feel worse.

11. You'd think dealing with pain on a daily basis would mean we always know how to manage it. Nope.

12. We don't want you to stop asking us to hang out. No matter how many times we have to say no!

13. Just because you haven't heard of our condition doesn't mean it isn't real.

14. We may not look sick, but we are sick.

15. We don't necessarily want sympathy; we just want acceptance. We just want our feelings and conditions to be validated by you and society.

16. We can't just take medicine and make it all go away.

17. More often than not, we want you to ask us about our condition. You will not upset us.

18. It may be a little difficult for us to listen to your adventures. But it's not because we don't care — because we want to have adventures of our own.

19. And most of all, we want you to know we appreciate you and everything you do.

Addendum F:
Linda in Coma, Date Unknown

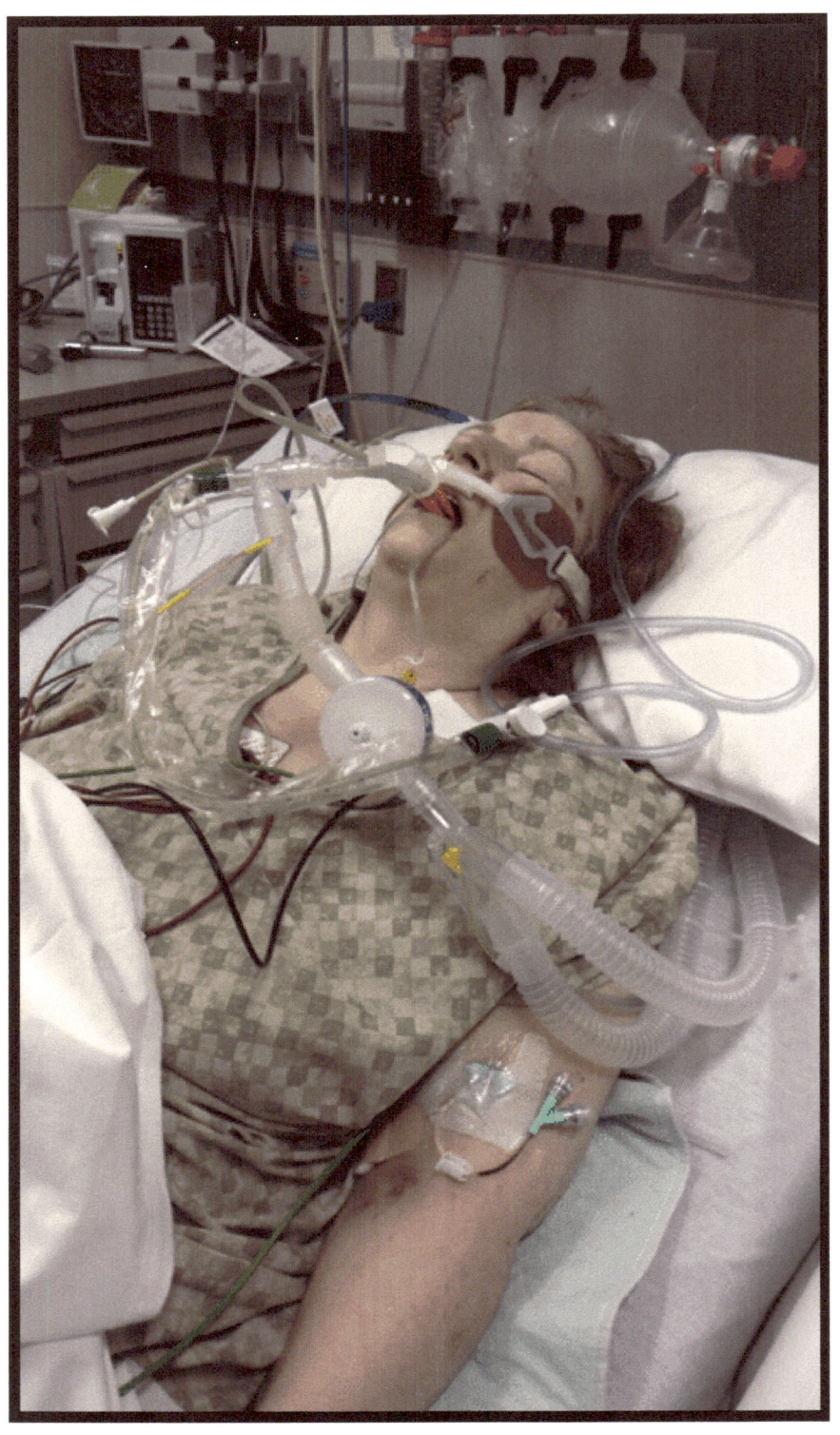

Addendum G:
Marketing and Photos of the Deadly Forest

Linda Diane Worthy Recalls her Ardouos Health Struggle and Journey of Faith in her Latest Work

"Freefalling... God's Angels By My Side" elevates the transformative power of heavenly help and steadfast hope during a perilous medical struggle"

News provided by
EIN Presswire
Feb 06, 2025, 3:25 PM ET
https://www.cbs42.com/business/press-releases/ein-presswire/783732519/linda-diane-worthy-recalls-her-ardouos-health-struggle-and-journey-of-faith-in-her-latest-work/

YORBA LINDA, CA, UNITED STATES,
February 6, 2025 /EINPresswire.com/

Author Linda Diane Worthy shares her extraordinary journey of survival and faith following her diagnosis of a rare and debilitating medical condition known as Bilateral Trigeminal Neuropathic Pain. In her latest powerful memoir, "Freefalling... God's Angels By My Side," Worthy recounts her battle through an unimaginable ordeal, starting with a failed sinus surgery in 2011 that launched her into a journey of spiritual and physical warfare.

At just 54 years old, Worthy faced a dramatic shift when the top neurosurgeon informed her that no medical treatment existed for her condition. Damage marred both sides of her face, and she received advice to live as fully as she could until her condition ultimately claimed her life.

The neurosurgeon acknowledged hearing of similar cases but had never met anyone with this rare condition. He urged Worthy to embrace life fully until the very end.

Against all odds, Worthy's story took a miraculous turn. She recounts her incredible survival through a series of documented events, featuring police, hospital, and eyewitness accounts, despite Intensive Care Unit doctors insisting she should not have made it. Amidst the pain and the looming shadow of death, her faith in God emerged as her unwavering strength. She witnessed miracles that defied imagination, including moments when she crossed over and returned "just in time."

This uplifting narrative emphasizes a medical journey that serves as a testament to faith, highlights divine intervention, and celebrates the unyielding love of God. Worthy aims to inspire those confronting life's toughest challenges to discover comfort in the assurance that God stands by them, providing His love and miracles even in seemingly impossible situations.

"Freefalling... God's Angels By My Side" by Linda Diane Worthy tells a gripping story of survival against all odds. It captures her steadfast belief in God's miracles and her profound gratitude for the divine guidance she encountered during her trials. Discover the shining wisdom and bravery that leap from the pages of this captivating masterpiece. Now available for purchase on Amazon, Barnes & Noble, Citi of Books and other major online bookstores worldwide.

CONGRATULATIONS!
YOUR BOOK IS NOW LIVE!

Selected by the New York Times Editorial Board for inclusion in an upcoming New York Times Magazine.

This year, Citi of Books was thrilled to be part of this vibrant gathering, where the love for literature was palpable in the air. Whether you were a lifelong bibliophile or a curious newcomer exploring the world of books, the festival provided a unique opportunity to connect with fellow enthusiasts and share our passion for the written word.

As we look back on this unforgettable weekend, we invite you to join us in reliving the highlights of Citi of Books' gallery during the 30th Los Angeles Times Festival of Books—a true celebration of the literary arts! A book included in the gallery was "Freefalling...God's Angels By My Side" by Linda Diane Worthy.

The Deadly Forest

Long slopes indicate drops of 100 or more feet where I fell in 2015 and 2017.

First Affirmation:

"When Friends And Family Reject You During Difficult Times."

I have lived this for over twelve years during my spiritual warfare, which even I didn't know about until God declared victory over twelve years later. I do try to be understanding about the many friends and family who unfairly judged me. I also was told by trusted people that I was not exactly nice when I got angry, usually from the terrible pain, while in an unaware state. Hmmmm..... The Hulk comes to mind! 😊

Because everyone knew I was experiencing one of the worst pains known to mankind year in and year out, based on a rare diagnosis from one of the leading neurosurgeons in the world, and because I would go in and out of unaware states (think Ambien), everyone assumed that I was crazy or mentally ill, except for a few friends and my precious dad who lived next door until his death in January, 2018, along with my neuropsychologist, who kept telling me I was NOT mentally ill; rather I was neurologically damaged from the failed sinus surgery in February, 2011.

I felt and heard my family and many friends' very low and hateful opinions of me. I have since forgiven them all. Mostly no response from those who refused to forgive. But, hey, as Christians, we know we seek forgiveness for us to walk with God.

One relative tried to take me to court and have me declared mentally insane to be stuck inside the state-wide mental institution (for life) where I would lose all my rights. Drive, marry, divorce, have money, vote, buy or sell property, etc. God was in control and the attorney was not intelligent enough to know I had to first be served before taken to court. So, I was never served, never knew about the court date, and thus my case was dismissed. God was not letting me be stuck in that kind of institution.

My neuropsychologist also was a weekly sounding board and reassurance for many years. Talk therapy was what I needed most.

Evil things were done to me, like the relative mentioned above lied to the hospital. I was refused the right to say goodbye or see my mom before or after her death, even though I was also in the hospital around the corner from her (*see Chapter Three*) as the hospital tried valiantly to get me breathing so I would even live. The entire family refused to tell me where my mom was even buried and no one had placed any kind of marker to indicate where she was!

I often asked God why. I felt lonely, abandoned, and despised and I had no idea why. Not once did anyone bother to go to the internet and research what long term non-stop intense pain with no cure can mean to the patient. Their personality changes for good. And not for the better.

I did a lot of solid medical research, but everyone refused to believe me or research it themselves. Have you ever felt so lonely and abandoned that you sometimes think ending your life was the only way left? Please don't act on those thoughts.

Have you ever felt that nothing you do or say matters? If you take prescription meds, do people call you a drug addict because they refuse to understand if your body needs those meds, there is no way medically for you to become addicted? They also accused me of being dependent on drugs, which is possible for some, but no one could explain why I always had extra meds left at the end of the month. That's because I only took them when I needed them.

Friends, it is a hard and lonely place to be when nothing you say or do is ever good enough. Even if you've lived a brilliant and fulfilling life before this happened to you, there can be simply no way to cope.

Many people did evil things to and against me, and only one person has ever apologized. But that's okay, because I know forgiving them is for me and my walk with God, regardless of what they do or say. No one bothered to show me love except my dad (and two friends). After my dad died, I was told grieving any longer than a month was childish.

Now, I don't know your experiences. But if any of mine sound similar to you, trust me. My heart cries for you. So. What do you do? Pray. Pray that God will lead you to a trusting friend (He did for me) who will listen to you, care about you, pray, send texts, calls or emails. Or even just meet for lunch.

Try not to dwell on what is happening. Be ready to forgive them when the time is right, but expect nothing from them. Keep a journal and try to write about happy memories so when someone is trying to destroy you, you can read your happy memories and know that once you were happy, and one day you will regain the strength to just ignore them and live your life as best you can.

It is so easy to want and fantasize revenge. Don't do it. Never forget God is always there for us if we are His children. And if I could survive the hatred and evilness while undergoing intense spiritual warfare, well, know that you can come out on the other side victorious.

I've shared some very deep and painful-beyond-belief things that I never put in my 1st Edition because I feel deeply my affirmations are to be pure and honest, and that they can bring hope and comfort to those who need it. If you need to talk, reach out to me at miraclesanddance@gmail.com. I will listen and respond as I check my email every day. I care.

God WILL see you through this in His perfect timing.

Second Affirmation:

What Do You Do When Everyone Thinks You Should Be Perfect And Feel Joyful All The Time?

I wrote a book about my twelve plus year intense spiritual battle. *Freefalling… God's Angels By My Side.* It took me 10 years to write it. God revealed to me mid-June 2023 that satan approached Him to destroy my so-called perfect life, and God gave him permission.

Between pain and rejection and too many heavily documented miracles to count, I think no one knew what to do with me. When in non-stop 24/7 pain for 10 years until I was prescribed a better pain med, I slept up to 20 hours a day to avoid the pain.

When in pain, one of the worst pains known to mankind, while going in and out of aware/unaware states (think Ambien) along with the pain that would somehow cause me to drop to the floor in a coma that could last hours or days, I found it natural in such pain to be a mean person, the total opposite of the real me.

I became hated, lied about, ignored, with only my dad to show me before his death in 2018, that he was the only one who ever loved me unconditionally. Very few people, family or friends, even bothered to try and understand the total angst I was going through year after year.

So, when I ask my question, "What do you do when everyone thinks you should be perfect and joyful all the time?" It's based on my journey, and my incredible miracle of dance that fills me with joy. It's like winning the lottery in a way. Everyone expects you to be this joyous person all the time. No one sees me when I still feel hurt and rejected at times. When I cry myself to sleep for various painful reasons.

When I go out in public, and if I feel depressed and I have to pretend like I feel joyous, when I just want to go home to bed and cry and to sleep, it can be a very hard life. Well, from the start I determined my affirmations would show the honest and real me. Extraordinarily blessed but still human. So you go to church and most people have their happy face on. Has this ever happened to you?

Some churches make it impossible to show in public that you feel that you're dying inside. Still, the mask remains. Has this ever happened to you? Sometimes it's just easier to stay home from church so you don't feel fake and you don't feel judged.

The only advice I can offer is find a close Christian friend of the same sex and meet with them to be open and honest. Never say too much until you know you can trust each other. Devise a code phrase that only the two of you know so if contacted by the other and they state the code phrase, you must take it seriously and find a private place, if possible, to listen to them.

Don't offer advice even if they threaten suicide. Ask if you can quickly and privately pray for them without judgment. Then pray. I had one friend who wrote out his prayers. I was so happy I could come back again and again and re-read what he had prayed. Then put and keep them on your daily prayer list, especially until the crisis has passed. It's hard to be on either side. I just think it's okay to show the real you without judgment.

I Cor 10:13 is my lifetime verse. *"No temptation has overtaken you except what is common to mankind. And God is faithful; he will not let you be tempted beyond what you can bear. But when you are tempted, he will also provide a way out so that you can endure it."*

Believe me when I tell you, God has used this verse in my life too many times to count. He will do the same for you if you simply ask Him to do so.

Third Affirmation:

How to be Grateful When You Feel Imperfect

From my own experience, I know how hard it is to be grateful when nothing is going right in your life. When you feel unloved and deserted, left alone and ignored. When you feel despised.

I'm no saint. I suffered greatly during my twelve plus years of spiritual warfare. I didn't even know that God was bringing me through it. God later told me that satan had asked God's permission to destroy me. Think of Job from the Old Testament. I have read that book several times because I feel strongly that some aspects of my journey resemble Job's journey, and it resonates with me.

Some people think I am "all that" because I wrote my book *Freefalling... God's Angels By My Side*. I most decidedly am not. I still stumble and fall in the Godly sense (not to laugh, but I also do this in the physical sense!!). There are days I feel unloved and angry at myself for blowing it. Yet again.

Not long ago, I was thinking about all of this, and I realized how imperfect I've been. And yet, God still loves me. He knows and loves me despite my damaged heart. Sometimes I feel guilty at how self-centered I was, just trying to survive. It was so hard. I'd feel guilty. Hated. Undeserving.

But I found I HAD to let go of these feelings at the altar of God. Still imperfect, I struggle... then I remember that God loves me and He will never leave me. Sometimes I have to keep remembering that despite my falls and imperfections, He still loves me.

Fourth Affirmation:

What's the Meaning of Success?

I believe there is no one set answer to this question. Based on our age, our upbringing, if we are a Christian or not, what are your earthly treasures, etc. Before my journey, I very rarely prayed or read the Bible. I just didn't think it did anything for me. By Biblical definition, I was a "lukewarm Christian".

Of course, by this time in my life (I turned 69 in July, 2025), I can look back and see how my opinions have changed over the years. God never changed. He never left me. He will always be my Heavenly Father.

The internet tells me: The idea that "God looks after the sparrow" is a common expression and a central theme in Christian theology, particularly in the New Testament. It emphasizes God's care and provision for even the smallest and seemingly insignificant creatures, highlighting the value of all His creation. The phrase often refers to Matthew 10:29-31, where Jesus speaks of sparrows being sold for a penny, yet none falling without God's knowledge. This verse is often interpreted as a reminder that God is aware of and cares for everything, even the most trivial things, and that His followers are infinitely more valuable.

This is a very comforting Bible passage, and usually takes away thoughts of not being sufficient in God's eyes, etc. It totally amazes me. Because if God considers the lowly sparrow to be important to Him, then how much more does God consider me HIS child? I can look back and recognize that God saw my heart. That even when I can seem to be utterly useless, God doesn't see me that way. Even when I don't feel it to be true, God does convince me it is true. I am His child. He does watch over me. I just need to follow His path.

So, back to success.

To some, it means making a lot of money. Or think of myself as greater than I ought. Success to me is being open and humble, to realize GOD gave me this book to write and share. For free (although I pay a great deal for each edition), as much as is possible. It means that I do not glorify myself at all during the remainder of my journey (until I die). To not think I'm "all that", but rather ask God to show me what HE wants me to do. To remain in His will no matter what.

The trouble, I think (and I am not rich so that could color my opinion), with monetary financial success is that it is not lasting for most people. They achieve a goal and not be satisfied and don't care as much for their family as they used to. Man or Woman. Woman or Man. And even children.

The bottom line for me is when I can see that I have been bragging is that I am 100% wrong and need to beg God for forgiveness, regardless of what others do or say. I don't try to live for myself or my reputation. God's got it in control. All of it. All the time.

Fifth Affirmation:

Why Me, Lord?

I believe that most Christians have asked God, regardless if nothing is going right, and even if God is blessing you right and left, why??? I know I have. It's ironic. While I went through twelve plus years of unbearable and unbelievable pain, death, abandonment, I cannot recall if I ever uttered those words.

Long ago, I placed my book Freefalling...God's Angels By My Side, at the feet of God. I purchased over a hundred books from my first publisher and paid to mail them or just give them to anyone who asked, and everyone I knew, even strangers.

Few people ever bothered to thank me. But, that is not important. God has spoken to my heart that this book will reach the world. Frankly, I am scared to death at the burgeoning success God is doing for this book. My unique journey. It sounds stupid to ask, WHY ME LORD?

I just looked at the growing number of five star reviews of my book on Amazon. It feels surreal. Like all these people are talking about me, and it feels as though they couldn't possibly be talking about me! And yet, I continue to ask God to keep me humble.

But why ME, Lord? I am nobody. I have sinned before God and family and friends. I am NO saint. But, God, You know my heart. All of it belongs to You. You have taught me the importance of truly forgiving those who have hurt me. More importantly, why I must seek the forgiveness and reconciliation of those whom I have wronged.

Sometimes, even family and former friends reject me, my journey, and how God has made me a new creature in Him. I feel profound shame at how I was. God is using this journey to glorify His name. I do and continue to praise Him for His many heavily documented miracles.

So, regardless if it is a good "Why me?" or a negative "Why me?", perhaps we should be asking, "Why NOT me, God?"

Linda Diane Worthy was à well known Washington state-wide "personality" as founder and co-director of Worthy Music Ministries in the 1990s and beyond.

Thousands of artists, bands, and choirs/ensembles came through Worthy Music Ministries through one or more of Chuck and Linda Worthy's annual Washington State Christian Talent Contests (1991—2011).

Saying Goodbye to Linda's parents in December, 2021

In her day job, she was a highly sought out senior software and application developer who was on most local recruiter's first-to-call list for someone with her skill set. Among her clients were Boeing, Microsoft, Dept of the Army, Department of Portland government (who oversaw six Oregon counties), Frank Russell, Weyerhaeuser, the Tacoma Events Commission, and far too many more to count.

Most kept calling her back for subsequent projects. She was brought in to fix the impossible. Because she was raised to think outside the box, she was successful in all her technical contracts and application development projects.

Linda also proudly served her country for seven years active duty in the US Navy as a Vietnam Era vet.

She received multiple awards for her many achievements, as well as for her many years in Civil Service before entering the private sector.

Raised to achieve whatever she put her hand to, she did not disappoint. She greatly desired to achieve her very best for her parents who had made so many sacrifices and given her such great encouragement: Earl Benson Jr. (1932-2018) and Beverly Benson (1936-2020)

Linda tries to please God in all she does, and to give Him alone the Glory for all He has prevailed against the enemy.

www.ingramcontent.com/pod-product-compliance
Lightning Source LLC
Chambersburg PA
CBHW040148120626
46344CB00034B/9